Little Bean's FUNDERWEAR DAY!

First Printing, 2014

ISBN-13: 978-0692021828

ISBN-10: 0692021825

SkinnyMinny Media LLC

info@littlebeanbook.com

www.LittleBeanBook.com

The images in this book are handdrawn using a sailor brush pen and then colored with copic markers on Borden & Riley #234 Paris bleedproof paper. All text is hand drawn.

The authors of this book are by no means experts when it comes to potty training. We don't have much experience in early childhood development, we aren't doctors or nurses or even childcare providers. WE ARE PARENTS. Parents who had (and in the case of Little Bean still need) to potty train. We know how challenging and frustrating it can be.

Funderwear Day is simply a celebration based on when you think your child is ready to take on the potty. When that time comes, pick a date on the calendar. Talk about it with your child. Read them this book. Have everyone in the family pick their "funderwear" and turn it into a celebration.

Once Funderwear Day arrives, diapers are no more. Your child has now graduated to wearing underwear. The first few days may be some of the most frustrating days of your life (be prepared with some good cleaning products on hand), but just keep reminding yourself, no one goes to kindergarten wearing diapers!

HAPPY FUNDERWEAR DAY!

--Roni & David

DEDICATION:

MY BOYS. MY INSPIRATION.
MY LIFE.

'To' Little Bean,
      it's time.

'To' Big Brother
      can't wait to see the Adventures of Super Ninja Droid

Shaina: for always being honest, pushing me to be great and being supportive

Lila: for telling me what I am doing is "cool" in the sweetest voice

Landon: For being a constant source of inspiration and always showing me another way of seeing

Mom, Dad, & Katherine: For constantly showing interest support & love.

Lee: For being the only person who could ever share my level of passion & enthusiasm.

This is Little Bean!

Little Bean was becoming quite A BIG BOY

He could walk

MOMMY MORE milk PLEASE
can i have cheese
we watch ICy movie
It's SUNNY OUT
we DO puzzle
He could TALK

He
could
STACK
blocks

and
ALMOST
put on his
OWN
socks

But there was ONE thing Little Bean didn't quite master

the
POTTY

Daddy
USES
the
potty

Even BIG BROTHER uses the Potty

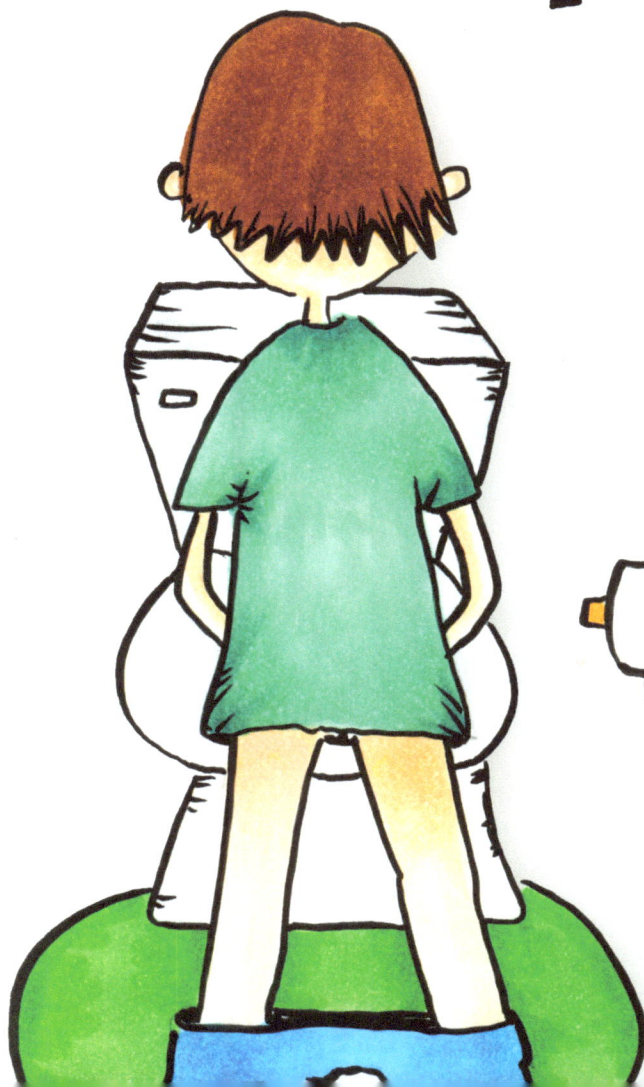

It was time for Little Bean to use the **POTTY** too!

On FUNDERWEAR
Day we all Wear
our favorite
Underwear

even YOU!

Dad likes his SANTA shorts

Even though it's not CHRISTMAS time!

Mom likes Purple and green stripes

Green is one of her FAVORITE colors

And BIG brother went with his favorite super hero

Super Ninja Droid

NOW it was Little bean's turn to pick

it was a hard DECISION

...but he finally found the PERFECT pair.

They had a SPACE ship on them

That night, Little Bean was VERY NERVOUS

He NEVER wore underwear before

but if Mom, Dad and BIG BROTHER
could do it, then so could he.

HAPPY FUNDERWEAR DAY!

www.ingramcontent.com/pod-product-compliance
Lightning Source LLC
Chambersburg PA
CBHW060816090426
42737CB00002B/81